HOW TO TALK TO SOMEONE... AND NOT DIE

A Handbook for Superheroes

LEE BURNS

ISBN: 9798682281879

Published by Clear Wind Publishing (USA)

TABLE OF CONTENTS

THE PLOT

As this is a *Handbook for Superheroes*, perhaps we should begin, as all good superhero stories do, with a bit of fantasy. . . .

Let's pretend for a moment that *you* are a superhero. Of course, as a superhero, you cannot die. Or at least, it's reeeeeaaaally hard to kill you. Sure, the form you are in may change, but the essence of what *is* you is pretty durable stuff.

Working off that premise, let's say your life extends well beyond the present one that you are in, both as far as you could imagine into the past, as well as an infinity into the future. Unless, of course, you stumble across an enormous amount of kryptonite, or something of the sort.

Your current circumstances, here on Planet Earth, have you trapped in a deep sleep. A state of hypnosis that you have endured for longer than anyone would care to recall. In fact, the daily pressures that you feel pushing in on you are the physical indicators of the continual *tic, toc, tic, toc* of "the hypnotist's hand watch," as it swings from side to side in the recesses of your mind, continually obscuring your knowledge of your past, your true future, and your superpowers.

So, what happened to you? How did you end up in such a state? Trapped in a prison of unawareness and supposed-to's? Mindlessly wandering through your days and your life. Numbed to the world around you, at large. Continually feeling disconnected, worried, and under the almost constant pressure that repeatedly shoves you back down, anytime you reach to be more aware.

Who would be so cruel as to sentence you to being unaware of your superheroness and powers, and why?

I'm sure you, as any rational person would, could wonder what you must have done to deserve such a fate. Surely, you must have committed some sort of crime. Prisoners aren't put behind bars, (even the ones in their own minds), without having done something wrong, something illegal, something criminal and terrible in the eyes of the law on whatever planet or galaxy they are in.

So, what *was* that law you broke? And what

was your superpower, anyway? Could it be that was what you were punished for, your superpower itself?

Oooohh, this is getting good! Yes! Yes! That's it! You were punished for using your superpowers. You were hypnotized into subjecting yourself to the invalidating bars that you then erected in your own mind, as only your own power would be strong enough to really trap you, since you're a superhero and all. I mean, nothing else could do it, right?

And then, then you were sentenced to forever walk unaware of your powers, or your lifetimes before and hitherto. You were locked away from the expanse of the galaxies and universes of material existence, stuck inside the head of a human meat body, out on the edge of all that is, on the prison planet of Earth.

Yeah. Yeah, that's what happened. Let's start our journey there. It's a good start.

Oh right, I almost forgot. You're probably wondering what your superpower crime was. Simple: you talked *to* someone.

CHAPTER 1

THE ANTAGONIST

I'm guessing that preface might not have been exactly how you were expecting a self-help book on communication to start. But, come on, who doesn't like a book that starts off by telling them they are a superhero? Ha!

Actually, I meant it. Completely and utterly. You are. And apparently a criminal, as well.

You ole troublemaker you.

So, let's get back to your crime: talking *to* someone. Did you know that it isn't possible to talk *to* someone without also being there? Just like you can't throw a ball to someone else or catch it when they throw it to you without being there in present time, where the throwing and catching is happening, you also can't talk *to* someone without being there in present time where the communication is happening.

You could be in the past, or be in the future, or

be somewhere else entirely, while you nodded to someone else's chatter, or waited for them to stop rattling on, so you could have your turn. You could throw out a bunch of ideas to someone else who is nodding absently or continually cutting you off or waiting for their turn to tell you how right they are.

But those would be talking *at* someone, not *to* them. And that, at least on the surface, seems to already be present in abundance on our planet. So, this book isn't about that.

Actually, *being there*, in present time, in the location you are in, with the person you are actually exchanging ideas with, also known as *communication*, is what this book is about. You know, talking *to* someone. Personally, I think two of the biggest problems we have in our world are that most people are not there and very few of us are truly communicating. It's a danger that is actually destroying our world.

Some years back, I was driving down a street in Burbank, California, around 1:00 am. I was teaching at an acting school at the time and had come from rehearsals of a series of 10-minute scenes that were all going to be performed for the public, in one evening.

In one of the scenes, two people were having a trying conversation in Central Park. The director of the scene had asked me to help out and play a homeless man who walked past the couple a few times and then later assaulted the man in the scene. The director had mentioned that he wanted the homeless man to "bring the danger" to the scene, even when he was just passing by.

I was going over this in my mind as I was driving home, when I spotted a homeless person. He was sitting under a covering at a bus stop. He had what I assumed were all of his belongings around him; bags, a cart, etc. He was wearing a tattered coat. No one else was anywhere around. But he was having a full-on argument with someone. And the thought struck me, "that's dangerous."

Think about it. If you were walking down the street toward that homeless man, who was having a full out-loud argument with someone else who obviously wasn't there, would you want to just walk up and say hello to him? Or even walk past him? Probably not. Probably you'd think about trying to cross to the other side of the street before you got to him. But why? What is so "dangerous" about a man sitting by himself, full-on talking at someone who isn't there?

Well, he obviously isn't being there, in present time. And he certainly isn't exchanging ideas with anyone who is also in present time.

If you were to walk up to him, maybe he'd pop into present time to some degree. Maybe he'd recognize that someone was there to talk to. But then again, maybe he'd think that you are the person he was arguing with. Maybe he'd try to attack you.

The problem is, since he isn't in present time, we don't really know what he's looking at, or who or what he is arguing with. So, we just don't know what he might identify us as or what he might try to do to us if we were to show up in the middle of the world that he is currently inhabiting in his mind, but not in his body. Thus, "that's dangerous."

When I played this homeless character in the performance, I incorporated what I had seen in real life. I made up someone that he was mad at from days previous. And as him, I shuffled across the stage, while arguing with that person, who wasn't there.

I had many, many members of the audience approach me afterwards to tell me how "scary" or "dangerous" that character was to them. And impactful. The director was thrilled, by the way.

Okay, well that's just a performance. What does art have to do with life, in this case?

Think back for a moment about a day in your past that was a great day. A really, really great day. Chances are, it was one where you were with someone or "someones" special, enjoying some type of mutual activity and exchanging ideas about it. You were probably really being there in both the space and time you were in, and in the activity that you were engaged in as well.

Or if it was a day actually spent alone, it certainly becomes more real and exciting when you share about that day with someone that you consider to be special. Plus, even alone it was still a day that you were really there, in the environment you were in, really involved in what you were doing. You know, really communicating with your environment.

Let me ask you this another way. Who is your best friend? Are they *there* for you? Are they willing to exchange ideas with you? Ideas about things that you both agree are real and important to both of you? Do you feel like they understand you? In other words, do you feel like they talk *to* you instead of *at* you?

And when you are with them, do you feel more alive? More *there*, in present time?

Well, what if you could make someone else feel that way? What if you could make anyone you chose feel that way, at least to some degree? That might be pretty special, wouldn't it? That might make a difference in our world. It certainly would in theirs. It might just save their day. Heck, it might just save the world. Hey! Maybe there's something to this superhero thing after all!!

And in sticking to our theme, then the evil supervillain would be the one who absolutely refused to *be there* and *talk to ANYONE!* Oh, what a nasty, dangerous villain! They probably hate everyone. And are probably trying to destroy the whole world by getting no one to be there and no one to truly communicate with anyone else.

They fight and want to enslave everyone. They don't talk *to* anyone, only *at* them. Many times, by yelling and threatening, but often also with a slivering tongue cloaked with a smile to cover their hate.

They obviously aren't in present time, because

they can't even see the person they are talking at. Not really, or they could see the good in them that superheroes like you can. They would know that humanity is worth saving, not destroying. Something one can only really know, by talking *to* humanity.

Of course, real superpowers can sometimes save even the worst of villains. So, let's dig a little deeper into these other worldly powers of *being in present time* and *talking to someone* and see where they might take us. Who knows, maybe that villain could turn out to just be someone who *really* needs someone to talk *to*.

CHAPTER 2
BEING THERE

When my two daughters were about six and eight years old, I took them to a fast food restaurant one evening for dinner. My wife and son were at a friend's house, watching movies, so it was daddy-daughters' time! One of my favorites!

Anyway, as we were in line, ordering and paying for our food, my daughters were very in communication with me, even loudly so, about what they wanted. And when they went to get into the booth they had selected, next to the window, they continued to be very verbal. I was grabbing the drinks at the drink fountain, and they were shouting to me across the restaurant to be sure to get their drinks, and ketchup, and napkins, and straws—and ketchup again; I mustn't forget the ketchup! I assured them I was getting everything and continued gathering the items and putting them on the tray with the food, while keeping an eye on them halfway across the restaurant.

They were both very lively in the booth next to each other. They were looking out the window and talking about what was outside and about playing on the playground soon. My youngest was putting her face on the glass. Then they were pressing on the booth and turning around in it, looking at the people in the booth next to it. My youngest was putting her mouth on the booth. You know, being there and communicating with everything; kid stuff.

I thought all of this was great, but I wasn't giving too much significance to it, as I sat down and sorted out the food and drinks AND KETCHUP. I was the best dad in the world, by the way, for getting all of this and especially the KETCHUP!

As my daughters continued their aliveness, touching the things around them, looking and talking, I noticed that there were others in the restaurant who were also noticing their aliveness and were smiling about it too. My daughters, of course, would smile back at anyone who they made eye contact with. Again, you know, normal kid stuff.

I was enjoying all of this when two teenage boys walked into the restaurant. One had on a ball cap, put on his head a little crooked, his pants hanging down with his boxer shorts partially hanging out. The other was similar, but also had headphones around his neck.

I watched the two of them shuffle up to the counter, order their food, pay for it, receive it, AND NEVER REALLY COMMUNICATE WITH ANYONE!!! They leaned their bodies back from the person at the counter and looked up at the sign or to the side, while they "told them" their order. And when the employee asked them if they wanted to "biggie size it" or whatever it was, they looked the other way and mumbled "yeah." When they were told the amount to pay, they looked down into their wallets, pulled out the money and tossed it on the counter, still looking away. When they got their change, they slipped it into their pockets and just slid down to the end of the counter to get their food.

As they stood and waited for their food to be delivered, they would look at each other and make little gestures or something, a short word or two exchanged, but nothing at all to anyone else. Then they got their food, shuffled over to the fountain and filled up their sodas, and shuffled to their seats. The one with the headphones had slipped them on by the time they both started diving into their food.

I sat in my booth, watching all of this in a state of shock, while screaming inside my head, "HOW IN THE HELL DID WE GO FROM WHERE MY DAUGHTERS ARE AT WITH *BEING THERE* AND *COMMUNICATING* WITH DAMN NEAR ANYTHING AND ANYONE, TO THESE TWO BOYS DOING ALL THEY COULD TO AVOID *BEING THERE* AND *COMMUNICATING* WITH DAMN NEAR ANYONE??!!!?"

HOLY NO TALKING TO ANYONE SUPERHEROES!! WHAT SORT OF VILLAINY ABOUNDS HERE?? Had a supervillain put some sort of spell on these boys, or had they hypnotized them? What prank was supervillainy up to???

While I didn't know for sure exactly what supervillainy abounded, it was clear that something was squashing life here and slowly choking out the flow of life—communication.

Have you seen this for yourself? Have you ever driven past an elementary school as it lets out? It's amazing to see these little ones come pouring out. It's incredible how much they are living in the moment they are in and how much they are in communication with it and with others.

If you haven't done this as an exercise, you

should. And then you should go to the high school and see the high schoolers coming out and see how hard they are trying not to be where they are in the moment they are in and to not be in communication with others. Perhaps you'll wonder as I did, WHICH VILLAIN IS RESPONSIBLE FOR THIS???

Perhaps you'll wonder as well if children show up as potential little superheroes when they first arrive. I mean, maybe they really do.

Have you seen what often happens in areas where it's mostly adults and a baby or child comes in? In nearly every area they pass through, life increases. If it's in a church, a restaurant, a waiting room, wherever, most of the adults they pass turn to look at the little one who can still be there and communicate.

"Now wait a minute, Lee!! Babies can't even talk!! What the heck are you talking about?"

Okay, okay. Fair enough. And if you'll stop yelling at me, I'll explain. Heh, heh.

I didn't say they were talking; I said they were communicating. Hugs communicate. Smiles do. Coos, gurgles, giggles.

Watch the next time you see a mom come through with a little one that is all alive and looking around at everyone. See how much the child grabs their attention. Watch those that the little one passes light up with smiles and how they sometimes make faces or wave or say hello to the little more-alive one.

Sure, some look away. Sure, some seem annoyed. Just more evidence of the supervillainy plague in action, if you ask me. And what is uplifting, what gives superheroes like you the hope to continue onward, is that *most* of humanity still recognizes life, and it still gives them hope and makes them smile or even communicate back to the little superhero in their midst.

CHAPTER 3
THE PROPOSAL

Okay, so what is it I am actually proposing here in this book, with all this superhero and being there and talking to people, communicating stuff? This is supposed to be a self-help book, for Christ's sake!

Well, you're right. Thank you for that communication.

If this is for self-help, then maybe we need to be more practical and real, and maaaaaybe just a little silly. I'll admit I've probably leaned a bit more on the silly, so far. So, here goes with practicality.

For now...

Sort of...

Since I started with you being a superhero and all, let's do a practical examination of a superhero first. What is the essence of what makes a superhero a superhero?

Well, if I was summing it up, and I am, I'd say that first off, they have powers that most others around them are not displaying. They can see things that others are missing, and they choose to do something about what they see.

Secondly, they want to do anything to fight off evil and to increase the survival chances of life around them. They believe in the good in humanity; they think the people are worth saving. Lastly, by their actions they give us hope for a better future.

So, how does *being in present time* and *talking to someone* tie into superhero type powers, in a practical sense? How important is that to life and livingness, anyway?

Well, let's look at it from another perspective.

What is used to threaten people into good behavior in nearly every area of this planet? The threat of imprisonment. Put plainly, getting thrown in jail.

But what's so bad about being in jail? Why do we feel our insides go into a frenzy when we see those flashing lights of the police car behind us?

Because he is connected to the power of law.

Law that could possibly put you in jail.

But again, what's so bad about jail? What does it really take away from you?

Well, it takes away your freedom.

But what is freedom?

Perhaps one large aspect of freedom would be your ability to determine where you will be and who and what you will interact or communicate with. Right? That could, in fact, be the largest and most important freedom there is.

And if they put you in jail, you lose that. You can't just hang out with your friends, or coworkers, or family and talk about whatever you want, whenever you want.

If you're in jail, you only get to be in the environment that they allow you to be in. You only get to talk to those that they allow you to talk to, when they allow you to talk to them.

And, other than death row, what is the worst thing they threaten the prisoners with?

Solitary confinement.

Other than being put to death, which certainly hinders your ability to be there and communicate, being put in solitary confinement is the threat that is used to get prisoners to behave. That or an extended sentence. Both of which further limit the prisoner's ability to be where they want and to be in communication with whomever or whatever they want. A most villainous threat, indeed.

To further the point, there is an infamous experiment that was done in the United States, in 1944, on 40 newborn infants. The infants were separated into groups of 20.

The first group had nurses who cared for all their physical needs but would do nothing else. No communication, no affection. Just meticulous physical care in a sterile medical environment.

Four months into the "experiment" it was cancelled as half of these 20 had died.[1]

Yes. Horrible, stupid villainy to be sure! And, as superheroes, we can and will do something to ensure that evil of this measure is not propagated again. That is part of the purpose of this book. So, steel yourself and let's press on.

Okay?

1 "US Experiment on Infants Withholding Affection." *Values Exchange*, stpauls.vxcommunity.com/Issue/Us-Experiment-On-Infants-Withholding-Affection/13213. (date accessed July 1. 2020)

CHAPTER 3

Okay.

There was no physiological reason for the babies' deaths; they were all physically very healthy. However, apparently before each baby died, there was a period of time where they would stop verbalizing and trying to engage with their caregivers, stop moving, crying, or even changing expression. Simply put, they stopped communicating. And once that stopped, life stopped shortly after.

Well what about the second group of newborns? In this group, they had the same type of medical and physical setting *and* communication and affection from the caregivers. Obviously, all of these babies lived.

Unfortunately, the dumbass villains running this "experiment in human behavior" had to have these babies die before being able to come to their "insightful" conclusion—that communication is actually a very vital need in humans.

The least they could have done was look into history, where apparently, back in the thirteenth century, the German king, Frederick II, conducted a similarly diabolical experiment intended to discover what language children would naturally grow up to speak if never spoken to. King Frederick took babies from their mothers at birth and placed them in the care of nurses who were forbidden to speak to them. And Frederick's experiment was also cut short because all of the babies died before they were able to speak any language.

In the 1970's the similar Harlow "pit of despair" experiments run on monkeys even had disastrous results.[2] Bottom line—you cut someone off from communication, and they decline to the degree that they are cut off.

Sorry. You wanted me to be practical. There you have it. In practical terms, we so desperately need someone else to talk to that the greatest threat we have held over our heads by the law is that we will have our freedom to do so taken away. And by experiment, we know that we actually can't live without it.

So, yeah, talking *to* someone saves lives. It increases the survival chances of life. It gives the lonely soul you are communicating to hope of

2 Kendra Cherry, "Controversial and Unethical Psychological Experiments for Research." *Verywell Mind*, May 10, 2020, www.verywellmind.com/controversial-psychology-experiments-2794997. (date accessed July 1. 2020)

something better, a reason to go on, an acknowledgement of their own value and confirmation that they exist.

And THAT, in my book—and this is my book—is superhero quality stuff. Period.

Flying and super-speed and super-punches ain't got jack on that. I'm sorry to go "dark" on you. It isn't how I like to communicate. But sometimes we need to take a minute to see the world as it is, to make a plan to help it. And from that plan, together, we can make right what a lonely few have wronged. Plus, you've seen or read the superhero stories, right? They always win in the end. So, I'm pretty confident in things turning out well in this story too, in the long run.

CHAPTER 4

THE POWER OF PRESENT TIME

I don't know if you've ever stopped to examine this one, but it is actually true that worry does nothing for you. It has no positive effect on the past or present. Its only real action is to steal the present moment from you, as your mind races away with possible negative scenarios in the future, usually from some past action, or lack of action, in some moment in the past.

Let's say you get pulled over for speeding. Your mind immediately shifts to the past and you start wondering what the officer clocked your speed at. If you had been able to slow down much before his laser gun hit your vehicle. Or, why didn't you slow down earlier? You thought about it for a minute, but then, your mind stuck on other worries, you spaced out, and forgot about your speed.

You wonder what you might say maybe to get out of the ticket, as your mind projects into the future for possible outcomes. That officer sure is staying in his vehicle a long time. Do you have a warrant out for your arrest? No way. No way. But is he mistaking you for someone else? What might happen if you do get a ticket? Will your insurance go up? Will your parent or significant other be mad at you? Can you afford to have your insurance go up, or be cancelled? Oh God, no, please not cancelled!

Meanwhile, in present time, none of these things are actually happening, despite the impending doom you feel in your stomach and pressure on your shoulders. I wonder, what would have happened if you *had* been in present time and not spaced out, worrying about the future, or replaying the past. Maybe, just maybe, you wouldn't have been speeding in the first place. Or maybe, just maybe, you might have seen the officer and been able to slow down enough to not get pulled over. Or maybe you would have been able to just be in present time, have a nice chat with the officer, and be let go with a warning, instead of a ticket. I know that has happened to me more than once.

In one such instance, I was driving in South Texas. I was thinking about getting home (the future) and was speeding along, not fully in present time. The next thing I know, I saw the flashing lights in my rearview mirror. I looked down at my speedometer and went, "Oh crap."

Only after I got pulled over to the side and the officer stopped behind me, did I realize it was a state trooper. I don't know how it is in your state, but in Texas, you almost never get out of a ticket with state troopers. So, when I realized it was a trooper, I just resigned myself to the ticket and relaxed into present time.

By the time that the officer was at my door, I already had the window down and my license and insurance in my hand. And after I handed it to him, he, of course, asked, "Do you know why I pulled you over?"

"Yes sir," I replied, "I was speeding. Sorry, man. Just wasn't paying attention."

To be honest, he seemed a little surprised at my honesty. And I'm not surprised. You see, I was a professional firefighter paramedic for a number of years. And during that time, I had a lot of calls I went on with the police. I gained a tremendous amount of respect for those guys back then.

Everywhere we went, as firefighters, everyone

was happy to see us. Everywhere the police went, there was nearly always someone who wasn't happy to see them. People were happy to talk to us. And most people were happy to lie to them. And, after seeing it over and over, I was amazed at how much they were able to keep their cool.

For example, I remember one domestic disturbance call that we went on, when I was the acting paramedic for that shift. There was a little woman, in her 40s, that the police had to spray with mace. I had her, and the officer who sprayed her, in the back of my ambulance for the ride to the hospital. The officer was a big, muscled up guy, who sat there calmly writing up his notes, while this little woman cussed at him most of the way into the ER.

She kept telling him he must think he's such a big man to mace a little woman, "Don't you, big man?!" she would demand. Each time, he would calmly respond, "No, ma'am. You attacked my partner, so you left me no choice." And then she would cuss him again.

The truth is that she had jumped on the back of the officer's partner, after repeated warnings to calm down. She was heavily intoxicated and totally NOT in present time.

After we dropped her at the hospital, I came back to the officer and told him I couldn't do his job, because I wouldn't be able to put up with that kind of continual verbal attack. And when I asked him how he did it, he calmly replied, "Oh, I don't worry too much about it. People get pretty upset in domestic disturbances. You get used to it."

Looking back, it's easy to see that he actually was in present time and wasn't worried about what had just happened in the past, or what might be done or said in the future. And that made it much easier for him to see this woman as someone who was just an upset person, so there was no reason for him to take what she was saying personally.

Well, if we take that back to my speeding incident, many years later, part of what I was thinking when the officer came up to my window was that this is just a guy doing his job. I was going too fast, and it's his job to keep the streets safe by correcting people who are doing that. Plus, I liked his cowboy hat.

And do you know that with me being in present time and treating him like a normal person, while respecting his position, he also saw me as a normal person, too?

I was driving a new Chrysler 300S, with the Hemi V-8 engine in it. And it was a good-looking automobile that would go fast. I called it my luxury, American muscle car. Or Maximus—Max for short.

Aaaaany who, the officer admired it too and started asking me questions about it.

Long story short, we had a nice chat and then he went back to his car. After making sure I didn't have any warrants out for my arrest, he came back and let me go with a warning.

"Wow that's great, Lee. So, your *How to Talk to Someone* book is teaching us how to get out of tickets? Do you guarantee this method?"

Uhhh, no, and no.

The point I'm making is that there is something powerful about being in present time, and sometimes there's even a little magic in it. If you're any kind of sports nut, I'm sure you've heard your superstar athlete talking about the game slowing down for them.

What's actually happening there?

They reach a point that they are so familiar with all of the elements and pieces of their game that none of it throws them into a state of worry about their past actions or the possible future outcomes. They are fully in present time; they see everything in one moment of play, and they simply play the game as it comes to them.

And it's pretty glorious and amazing to behold too. We sometimes consider them to be heroes for their ability to do this. Or is it superheroes???

Huh?? Huh???

Ha! You knew I just had to throw that in there, didn't you?

Anyway, back to the point. Let's really look at this for a minute. Did you know that the only moment you actually exist in IS present time??? Sure, you have great memories and great future plans. But you *exist* in the present moment. And that moment is where you examine the past or plan the future from.

When you were creating those moments that are now great memories, those were times when you were really IN present time. Your attention was there, and you were enjoying the moment. And when you are creating—not worrying about but *creating* any good future that comes to manifestation—you are doing it *from* present time.

The way I look at it, present time is the foundation for actually living life. Factually, it is the only place you are in, and it is the only place you are experiencing from. And if you are really going to talk *to* someone one, instead of *at* someone, it's the only place you can do it in, as you and they are factually not in the past or future, regardless of where your attention is at.

The problem is, on this crazy planet called earth, with all of our modern-day pressures and problems, it can often seem really hard to keep your attention in present time.

The constant barrage of commercial and media-based messaging pushes all of these ideas of what you are supposed to be, what you are supposed to have, what you are supposed to do in order to just be happy and accepted, to the point that you become a hamster on a wheel. You're running like mad but feel like you're not really getting anywhere. And the gnawing pressure of the cage just keeps building.

I bet that wheel was built by a supervillain. A trap of images that keep you running from the past and chasing the future, while completely missing the present moment where you could step away from that wheel and walk right out of the open door of your cage.

But just in case you've forgotten your super-powers and feel like you can't quite muster up the strength to just fly off that wheel and into present time, I've written some additional chapters to help you build back up your superpower muscles.

CHAPTER 5

YOUR ADMIRATION MUSCLE

Have you ever sat and stared at a painting you admired? A sunset? A newborn baby or the face of your lover? Have you ever gotten the autograph of your favorite athlete? Or had a quiet chat with a parent or grandparent who really influenced you? Have you walked into your first house, or dream house, or apartment, or treehouse, with excited awe? Have you driven your first car, or ridden your first motorcycle or your favorite horse, that you really connect with?

Have you stood at the side of the road and watched soldiers or first responders walk by? Did you marvel at humanity as strangers from around the world all rushed into Ground Zero to help other strangers after 9/11, while the whole world grieved as one and then lifted each other back up again?

Has your child, or dog, or cat, or bird, or hamster greeted you with a nuzzle and made your heart melt and your knees buckle, as your bad day faded away and you became lost in their heart and kindness?

Or have you simply ever really, really enjoyed an ice cream cone on a hot day, the wind through the trees, or the moving timbre of your favorite singer's voice and just felt totally pleased?

If the answer to any of the above, or a million other possible examples, is yes, then I have great news for you! You still have an admiration muscle.

Checkmark!

You're a superhero!

You must be, since you obviously have their most powerful strength.

Admiration is defined as the feeling of wonder, approval, or pleasure. Of course, it comes from the root word admire. And admire has its origin in Latin, from the word *admirari*, which means 'to wonder at, to admire.'[3]

---

3 Mahoney, Kevin D. "Latin Definition for: Admiror, Admirari, Admiratus." *Latin Definition for: Admiror, Admirari, Admiratus (ID: 1163) - Latin Dictionary and Grammar Resources - Latdict*, 2020, latin-dictionary.net/definition/1163/admiror-admirari-admiratus.(date accessed July 1. 2020)

CHAPTER 5

You know what one thing all superheroes seem to have in common?

They admire humanity. They believe in what it is capable of. They see something worth saving in them because of the hope of what they can become and the goodness of who they truly are, deep inside. The supervillains are always saying there is no reason to help humanity. They point out its greed, its selfishness, its destruction. But the superheroes always counter with the beauty they've seen in the people around them, or at least know is possible within them.

I know, I know. I said I would be practical. So, I will. When you are admiring someone or something, you certainly can feel "at wonder," or at least in a state of pleasure or approval, no doubt. But what I find just as amazing, and what is important to us in the use of knowing how to talk *to* someone, is the power that admiration has to connect you to things in the present and pull you into present time. I'll give you an example of this by talking about someone I've admired in my life, my grandfather.

My grandfather passed away in 2011. Probably to return to the great hall of superheroes in the sky, or their home planet or something.

Here is an excerpt of a post that I wrote and shared on social media to honor him, several days after his funeral.

What I Learned from My Grandfather

My grandfather recently passed from this life. And I, as I am sure many do at times like these, looked back on time spent with him to see what I remembered most about him.

My most vivid memory is his greeting to me, each and every time I saw him throughout my life. "Hey Lee-Boy!" he would always enthusiastically exclaim. The thing is, though, he didn't just greet his grandson this way. Ask anyone who knew him, and they will tell you he greeted anyone who entered his door with enthusiastic acceptance and love.

When my uncle-in-law, Bill, spoke at the funeral service, he said that when he met my grandfather, he was instantly made a part of the family. But Bill also said that, within five minutes, he also knew where my grandfather's priorities were: God, family, country, and then his other groups, (the Texas Rangers, Dallas

*Cowboys, and Dallas Mavericks),
and he was a staunch defender of
every group he considered that he
was a part of.*

*I think it was not by coincidence
that my grandfather was one of
the happiest people I have known,
even though he lived the last twenty
something years of his life with very
limited use of half of his body due
to the stroke he had suffered. But
he rarely complained. Instead, he,
in typical Papa fashion, preferred
to find the good in his situation and
focus on that. Which is how he dealt
with everyone he knew, as well. He
never focused on the bad deeds
or offense of another, but instead
would defend their good qualities,
both to them directly and to anyone
who would bad-mouth another, even
if the person being bad-mouthed
wasn't around.*

*So, what did I learn from my grand-
father?*

*I think a real insight into happiness
and greatness.*

My grandfather didn't treat people

*the way he did or give allegiance
to his groups to the level he did
because he was a happy person.
No, he was a happy person because
of the integrity he lived his life by.
Because he chose to love others
and build them up instead of tearing
them down. Because he saw it as a
duty to support every group he was
part of.*

*Certainly, no man is perfect and nor
was my grandfather. But I can hon-
estly say that he worked most of his
days to see and celebrate the good
in others.*

*Thank you, Papa, for showing me a
real secret to life and happiness.*

Love, LeeBoy

As the note obviously makes clear, I admire
what I consider to be my grandfather's secret to
happiness, greatness, and maybe life itself. But
more to our point here, what does that have to do
with your muscle and being in present time?

Well, when I was with my grandfather, I was
almost always in present time. Even when I was
only a little tyke on a horse with him, out call-

ing the cows in from the pasture with a heartfelt "Suuuuiiiiii, cow!" that would get them on the trot towards the barn, I was fully there. When I was a boy of 12 or so and we were fishing, I was there. And even when I became a married family man myself and would pop in for a visit or to mow his and my grandmother's yard for them, I was just there, hanging with my Papa. It was a relaxing thing to do. It made me feel more alive. It made me more there in the moment where I am alive— present time.

But he's not the only one. I also admire my grandmother for her love and her cookies and her prayer-stained knees, my father for his never-ending drive to provide and help, my mother for her boundless energy and how she rides a Harley, my wife for her caring and kindness and for putting up with me, and my brother for his heart and smile. I also admire each of my children for their very different but very incredible strengths and for their willingness to have their own view of the world. In fact, there is no family member or friend that I have that I do not have multiple things about them that I admire.

And with each of them I have so many moments when we have shared present time and a nice talk to each other.

You know who else I admire?

YOU!

Yeah, YOOOOUUUUU!!!

You're still reading. You're still moving forward. Despite the spinning wheel in your hamster cage and the pressures of this "prison planet." Despite being "trapped in a meat body" and not being able to remember your superpowers, you *are* continuing forward. Being able to persist on any course that you are on takes real power and focus. And here you are, persisting. THAT is worth admiring.

I don't know if you've ever considered it, but despite what the worry in your mind might tell you, you are getting more right than wrong. Otherwise, you wouldn't still be here.

So, let's take your stick-to-it-ive-ness and start applying it in the coming first exercise.

CHAPTER 6
EXERCISING YOUR ADMIRATION MUSCLE

For the next three days, or five days, or seven days, (your choice), you are to work out your admiration muscle each day. Don't worry, we'll start with baby steps. The important thing is that whatever number of days you pick, stick to it all the way to the end. Use your stick-to-it-ive-ness superpower and keep going. And if you fall down (accidentally skip a day), don't worry about that. All superheroes fall down. But they all get back up, too, and so can you.

EXERCISE:

Go for a walk outside, or if weather doesn't permit, in a mall, or even your own house or work office and find things in the environment that you admire. Perhaps it's a tall building, or nice landscaping, or a large tree that seems to have been in a particular spot for a very long time, or maybe even one that's just starting to sprout. It can be a piece of concrete, a beautiful car, or moped, or bicycle, or motorcycle, or clouds in the sky, or, or, or.... Anything that you look at and you get a sense of wonder, pleasure, or even just approval for.

The important thing isn't what you look at to do the exercise, it's that you DO the exercise. Keep walking, keep looking, keep noting the things you admire until you feel like the world isn't quite doomed for eternity. Until you crack a smile, or maybe even a laugh. Basically, until you feel a little better, or a lot better, than you did before you started the exercise.

> **NOTE:** It is possible that you might feel a little worse when you first start than before you began. Don't worry about it, ignore the butterflies in your stomach and just keep going. Just like sore body muscles have to be loosened up and conditioned, so does your admiration muscle.

WHAT TO DO:

After you finish your walk, note down all the things that you can remember admiring.

[If you'd like a free pdf of this exercise, and

all the rest of the exercises, to print out for easier writing, go to www.handbooksfor-superheroes.com and enter the passcode: someone.]

THINGS YOU ADMIRED:

DAY ONE

_____

_____

DAY TWO

_____

_____

DAY THREE

_____

_____

DAY FOUR

_____

_____

DAY FIVE

_____

_____

DAY SIX

_____

_____

DAY SEVEN

_____

_____

DAY EIGHT

_____

_____

DAY NINE

_____

_____

DAY TEN

_____

_____

Did you complete your selected number of days on the exercise?

Great!

Well done!

It's time for the next step!

If you did not complete your days, it is very important that you do so. Each of the exercises in this book is built one on top of the other, to recover/rebuild and strengthen your superhero muscles. If you were going to try to run a marathon, you wouldn't make it if you skipped to the starting line and just took off with the sound of the gun. You'd have to have done the training to endure. You'd have to have stretched out each day, ran when you didn't feel like running, pushed through when you didn't feel like pushing through. You would have had to have used your stick-to-it-ive-ness superpower to make it through all the training.

Sure, there would have been days that you felt like you were in too much pain to run. There would have been days where you had to rest and heal and let the body recover. Days when you would have learned to push through and days when you would have just not been able to.

But if you had gotten back to it when you stopped for a day, or a week, or a month, and if you actually *did* all the training required, you could have built up to the point of running that marathon. Heck, maybe you could have even won it.

The same thing could be said about this book. If you *do* the exercises, you will arrive at being able to talk *to* someone. This is our first exercise. It's an important foundation. To build up to talking *to* someone you will need to have this foundation.

So, if you haven't fully done this first exercise, please don't go on to the next chapter yet. Pull your superhero cape out of your closet, put on your walking shoes, possibly some tights, and get out there and admire! Trust me, you'll be glad you did. And who knows, you might even find that you admire present time.

CHAPTER 7

ADMIRATION AND YOU

Quick, tell me ten things that you admire about yourself. Go!

"Holy crap, Lee! Don't throw us into the deep end of the pool without any warning or at least showing us how to doggy paddle in it!!!!"

You're right. My bad. Let me try this again.

Why do you think it is so hard to for most people to find things they admire about themselves? I mean, it's not a unique disease, this illness of self-invalidation that keeps you from remembering and using your superpowers. It seems to be a rampant, worldwide infestation!

Conversely, as one of my favorite acting teachers, Eric Matheny, used to say, "No baby shows up thinking, 'Oh my God, I'm so fat. I've got to lose some weight.'"

And they don't, do they?

Come to think of it, they also don't hate others because of their differences in skin color or genitalia or voting records or belief systems or financial solvency. And they also don't hate themselves or anything about themselves. They just sit there in their diaper, or even naked, in present time, doing whatever it is that they are doing, with no real attention on themselves.

Interesting, isn't it?

Cut to some 17–18 years later and observe that baby now coming out of the high school, and we're very likely to see someone that is filled with self-invalidating thoughts and all kinds of attention flowing inward on themselves, as opposed to interest in the world around them.

How does this happen? Was it really a super-villainous spell that has been pushing us down since birth? Or is it perhaps a rigged society or system? Is humanity really an evil race, filled with inner hate and destructive tendencies?

Without following Alice, or Neo, or anyone else down rabbit holes that aren't really of benefit to us in this particular adventure, it doesn't take much observation to see that for whatever reason, our society isn't currently creating an abundance of free thinking, confident, and caring superheroes.

So, how can we reverse that? Turn off the ever present, self-invalidating thought machine that continually tells us we are wrong or aren't good enough? Well, perhaps we can start with a really good, honest look at ourselves and WHAT WE ARE GETTING *RIGHT!*

Did you know that you made it to the end of your day to read this chapter, or the beginning of the next day to pick up the book again, or whatever point it is in your day that your eyes are following these words on this page?

Somehow, you made it through all the yesterdays before and the hours and minutes leading up to this moment now.

How did you pull this off? You must be a superhero!

"Oh, stop it, Lee. It's no big deal!"

It isn't?

Are you sure?

Have you looked at how difficult it can be to make it through this world? How many pressures are pushing in on us on a daily basis? From the

LEE BURNS

time we could put our eyes on screens, nearly every advertiser has been telling us how our life is incomplete or filled with problems without their product. How we are not beautiful enough, skinny enough, muscled enough, rich enough, or smart enough.

Our 24-hour news program channels shove constant disaster and fear and hate and impending doom at us from every angle of the world. The talking heads on so many of our talk shows bicker constantly about how our society is wrong, or this celebrity shouldn't have worn a particular piece of clothing or voiced an opinion, or how the athlete of the day is selfish, or how they shouldn't have taken that shot or thrown that pass or kicked that ball or, or, or...

If you're in school, you've got to balance all of the rest of your life around study and giving back to the instructor the answers they are looking for. If you're out into the work-a-day world, you've got to spend your time making your boss happy in order to keep your job.

And if you're trying to advance yourself, you may even have to be doing both at the same time! And if you're an entrepreneur, then you are part of the group that is crazy enough to be willing to work and worry 24/7/365 in order to not have to be a "40-hours-a-week slave."

And what if you're a mom AND have a job or business to run? How many plates do you have to be able to spin to pull that off??? Or a dad who is working two or three jobs so that your wife can do the job she loves most in taking care of the kids and providing a loving home for them to be nurtured in???

Meanwhile, regardless of which game you are playing, you've definitely got to work out more, make more money, save it better, have better skin, be more positive, eat healthier foods, drive a better car, wear better clothes, be a better person of faith, post it all on social media to prove it, and always, always, ALWAAAAAYYYS keep working to be more, be better, be more, be better, BE MOOORE, BE BETTEEEEEERRR!!!!

Or is that all just what used to go on in my head???

No?

You've noticed it, too?

Okay, good. I get tired of being the only one. Ha!

So, again I say, do you realize that somehow you made it through all of the yesterdays before and the minutes or hours leading up to this moment now, despite all the voices out there and the ones inside your head?

Aaaaaand you are still here???!!!

Let's not just leave it at that, either!

Let's take a good look at some of your other actions leading up to this moment, other than *just* arriving to it. You've handed out kindnesses to others along the way, haven't you?

You've held open doors for strangers, brought cupcakes or donuts to work or school. You've said prayers for others, you posted supportive comments to your friends on social media, visited loved ones in the hospital. You've shared funny posts that brightened others' days. You've donated old clothes, cooked warm meals (or at least picked them up through the drive-through).

You've bought birthday cards, sang songs, danced to tunes.

You've held others close as they cried over their losses. You've raised up their chins and told them things would get better. You've carried groceries for a neighbor, given a smile or directions to a complete stranger. You've shown someone how something worked to help them be better at an activity. You've coached and cheered baseball teams and soccer teams and all kinds of other teams, making those on the field, the mat, the court feel that they matter.

You've loved another. You've lost love and carried on. You've lost loved ones and carried on.

You've voted to support causes you believe in. You've donated time and money to causes that help this world become a better world.

You've painted a wall or a piece of furniture or a picture. You've petted a dog, a cat. And you've done a million other kindnesses and acts of help that stretch around the world and actually *are* the things that keep it running. And, believe it or not, at times, maybe just a few times, but at times, you've looked in the mirror and thought, "I look goooood, today!"

You've started on that diet, again, because you're worth having good health. You've read another self-help book, because you know that better is inside of you, so you've reached out to get it. And not because *they* say you should, not because of the pressures or the push of external forces. No. Not because of any of those. Because *you* desired to be the truest version of yourself for *you*.

Well, how in the hell did you pull this off???

I, for one, can come up with no other conclusion than to return to my initial analysis—YOU *MUST* BE A SUPERHERO!!

Seriously!!

You know what one of the biggest qualities that every superhero I can think of has?

They keep going!!! They pick themselves back up! They keep going toward their goals and dreams, no matter the disaster around them, no matter the pain they are in. They keep hoping in a better tomorrow. They keep fighting to make a better world, because they believe more in the beauty and hope around them than in what their archnemesis is telling them to see.

And that all starts with admiring what is out there. But what really pulls it off and keeps you in present time enough to fight off the supervillainous spells that have been cast over this world is turning the power of that admiration muscle on yourself.

However, before I turn the baton over to you, I'd like to take it for a spin and tell you what I see.

There is no person alive that is not deserving of love. There is no person alive that doesn't matter. There is no person alive that cannot heal. And no matter their current place in this world, there is no person that cannot start again.

If no one has ever told you, I for one am glad that you are here. I'd like to keep you. I think you have amazing strength and beauty inside you; that is the deepest part of you. I think you have extraordinary love inside of you, that is the truest part of you.

We all have superhero powers within us. We all can rise up. We all can make a beautiful present time, together.

The world needs your help. It has placed the spotlight in the sky, emblazoned with your superhero emblem, and is anxiously awaiting your reply. It's time for you to come to the rescue.

And the first person who needs rescuing may be YOU.

So, pull on your tights and cape and let's get to it.

Onto the next chapter and exercise, right after you wipe your eyes.

I know, I know. It's just allergy season. No biggie.

You ole softie you.

Heh heh.

Don't worry, I am too.

So, I guess we're in this together. To the end!

CHAPTER 8
EXERCISING ADMIRATION OF YOU

What is one thing we know about all famous superheroes? That they have an archnemesis. So, of course, you being a superhero and all; you have one too.

Do you know who it is? No, it's not you. It's the part that isn't you. The part that was taught, drilled, pressured, and coerced into you. That super evil archnemesis—self-invalidation! And THIS is the chapter where we build up our superhero muscle so big that we can eventually look that arch-nemesis square in the eye and not even flinch!

For the next three days, or five days, or seven days, (your choice), you are to work out your admiration muscle *on yourself* each day.

Wait, wait, wait!

Don't put the book down!

Don't throw it in the trash either!

I'm telling you; you want to do this!

And you CAN do this!!!!

Remember, in the last chapter, all of those wonderful things that we went over that you have already done before arriving at this moment?! Remember how much the world needs you and your superheroness?!

I bet if you stop and think right now, there is someone in your life that you have noticed is suffering under the pressure of the supposed-to's of this planet. And knowing you, you probably wanted to help them. Aaaand maybe you're wondering now, "Well, yeah, Lee, but what the heck does me admiring myself have to do with me helping someone else? This is stupid."

First off, ouch! Secondly, oooooooh but it has EVERYTHING to do with YOU ADMIRING YOU!

Suppose I was to come up to you on the street and ask you for one hundred dollars. And suppose you really wanted to give me that one hundred dollars.

Hey! I like where this is going! Let's stay on this one! Ha!

Okay, back to the analogy—I ask for one hundred and you want to give me one hundred.

But what if you don't have one hundred dollars? Even if you deeeeeesssssperately wanted to give me that one hundred dollars, if you don't have it, you can't. Period. And that's no good for both of us!! Especially ME!! This is pretty simple to understand, right? You can't give me what you don't have. But let's say you had one thousand dollars. Or one million dollars, even.

"Hey, Lee! I like where this is going! Let's stay on this one! Ha!"

Okay, stop copying me, so I can continue.

Anyhow, obviously if you have one million dollars, giving me one hundred of it would be incredibly easy for you to do, wouldn't it? You wouldn't even feel it. You'd probably have a few thousand in your wallet anyway. So, giving away one hundred is something you could do without really even thinking twice about it. You'd be so used to having and handling money that it would be an easy thing to give and receive.

Well, what if I was down on my luck and really having a hard time with life and just couldn't see my way out of it? And what if I just needed someone to see the good in me? To help me see the good in me. To give me an ounce of admiration over just one thing that was worth approving about me.

And what if you were so used to walking around in a state of wonder about yourself and the world around you? Or at least used to looking at things with a sense of pleasure and finding what you approve instead of what you wish were different or what you want to tear down, even with yourself?

Maybe if you walked by me on the street, maybe you'd have a million admiration-dollars in your account. And maybe you'd have a hundred or so you could spare on me.

And maybe, just maybe, this would be a superhero moment in my life that gives me hope again. That gets me to see that I can get something right. That I can be worthy of approval or that I can cause another to be pleased or possibly, maybe, at least for a second or two, to have some sense of wonderment.

The truth is, deep down, we all want to help someone that way. And there are few things that help another more than seeing the good in them. So, let's start by practicing seeing the good in us first ... beginning with you.

Now, back to our drill. For the next three days, or five days, or seven days, (your choice), you are to work out your admiration muscle *on yourself* each day.

The important thing is that whatever number of days you pick, stick to it all the way to the end. Remember, you can use your stick-to-it-ive-ness superpower and keep going. And, as always, if you fall down, (accidentally skip a day), don't worry about that. We know that all superheroes fall down and that they all get back up, too, and so can you.

EXERCISE:

Each day, as you go about your day, notice what you get *right*.

Maybe you put your shoes on the right feet or that you poured coffee in a cup instead of a wine glass. It could be that you hugged your kid before they left for school or called your mom to say hi. It could be that you let someone in front of you in traffic or that you just look goooooood today. That you smiled at a stranger or really helped a customer. That you said prayers for someone in need or posted something in social media that made others smile or feel good. Or it could be that today was a really, really, really tough day and that somehow you managed to get through it, anyway.

It can be anything that you can look at and feel like you could approve of in yourself. Anything you did or simply are that you feel pleased about. And maybe, on those really special days, it could even be something that makes you stand back in wonder of yourself and all your superheroness.

The important thing isn't what you notice about yourself that is right, while doing the exercise, it's that you DO the exercise. Keep noticing your kindnesses or perseverance, your ability to do the right thing, whatever is right about you until you feel like you aren't quite doomed for eternity. Until you crack a smile about yourself, or maybe even a laugh of wonderment.

At the end of each day, if you think you can't find even one thing that you got right, remember that you made it to that moment. And if that doesn't get you to at least see THAT as something to be admired about you, then go back and read Chapter 7 all over again. As a matter of fact, anytime that you come to the end of your day while doing this exercise and can't find something to write down, go back and read Chapter 7 again. Then come back here and write down at least one thing that you can admire about yourself.

> **NOTE:** Just like in our previous exercise, it is possible that you might feel a little worse when you first start than before you began. Don't worry about it, ignore the butter-flies in your stomach or hammering in your head and just keep going. Like sore body muscles have to be loosened up and con-ditioned, so does your admiration muscle. Especially when you are using it against your archnemesis—self-invalidation.

WHAT TO DO:

Throughout the day or at the end of each day, write down all the things that you got *right*. In other words, what you did that is worth admiring. Or simply skip to what you managed to admire about yourself today and write those things down.

> [If you'd like a free pdf of this exercise, and all the rest of the exercises, to print out for easier writing, go to www.handbooksfor-superheroes.com and enter the passcode: someone.]

THINGS YOU ADMIRE ABOUT YOU:

DAY ONE

_____

_____

DAY TWO

_____

_____

DAY THREE

_____

_____

DAY FOUR

_____

_____

DAY FIVE

_____

_____

DAY SIX

_____

_____

DAY SEVEN

_____

_____

DAY EIGHT

_____

_____

DAY NINE

_____

_____

DAY TEN

_____

_____

Did you complete your selected number of days on the exercise?

Great!

Well done!

I admire you for making it through this step!!

CHAPTER 9
STRANGER DANGER

What is it in us that causes us to tear down others that we don't know? I mean, why do we often look for what's wrong in others, instead of what's right? As we know, babies don't show up doing that to themselves. And they don't show up doing it to other babies either. When you were growing up, were you taught not to talk to strangers?

Of course, you were. Otherwise, you'd still be talking to them!

Maybe it starts with our well-intentioned parents and teachers telling us not to talk to strangers because they might take us away. I mean, it was probably a needed protection, even though the statistical chances of that happening are staggeringly small. I think we can all agree that this happening once in the history of the world is one time too many.

Now if that was the only time we were told

about stranger danger, maybe we would have gotten past it. Maybe we would have known to just avoid creepy dudes giving out candy from a van. But those aren't the only ones our minds seem to crave finding the wrong in.

Perhaps it was the invention of news or political parties or certain kinds of talk shows that spurred it on in our parents, before it was passed down to us. Or maybe it's just the constant barrage of the "not good enough," "never live up to it" pressure of this place.

Whatever the origin of the disease, at least the cure is clear.

TALKING *TO* SOMEONE!!!

Let me ask you this, have you ever been part of a school or a party or church or work group where there was a "general consensus" or "everyone knows" view of the bad character of one of the people in the group? And have you ever had the experience of somehow eventually ending up talking to that person and finding out that, "Hey, this guy or gal isn't so bad, after all!"?

I bet you have. And I bet that if you haven't, after you finish this book you just might have enough superpower muscles rehabbed to do so.

Even if you haven't had that experience yourself, I'm sure you know of a time when it happened with a friend, as part of a group or the ostracized person themselves. Maybe it was even one of those great times where the superhero that talked to that person had enough strength to share this new, more accurate view of them with the rest of the group and turn the whole group's view of this person around. A move so powerful that it probably also turned that person's life around, too.

It's quite extraordinary to me how many times these types of things happen, where we find out the new kid in school or the new person on the block or the worker at our job, or, or, or turns out to not be nearly as bad of a stranger as we first thought them to be.

Did you know that you couldn't be reading this book without the help of all kinds of good-willed strangers? Seriously.

For you to be reading these words right now, there's a whole list of strangers that contributed to get it to this point. First off, I had to write it. You're welcome. Then my editor had to edit it. Dear Lord, thank you, Sarah. Someone had to help with the layout of the book, someone had to design the cover that got your interest. Put it in the store or online.

If you're reading it on paper, then a whole series of folks were involved in getting the material—tree, tree pulp, recycled papers—and turning it into this paper. There's the whole process for the ink. What about the person who invented that? Or even who came up with this font that helps my personal style and concepts communicate to you?

Yes, I have a personal style, stop laughing.

Aaaaanyway, we haven't even gotten into the location that you are reading it in and the electricity it takes to run the lights in it or the coffee that you sip while you read it, or, or, or, or …

And don't think you got out of it if you're reading an eBook. What about all the strangers that contributed to the device you're reading on? And who designed the app that makes it so that the lighting in the device and behind the words and paper makes it seem like you are actually reading a paper book, while also emphasizing the layout and font that helps to communicate my style?

I do to have a style!!

But to the point, if you're starting to get a glimpse of this chain of helping strangers that made this whole conversation you and I are having possible, just stretch that out to your drive to work or school today, the breakfast you ate on the way, the street the car or bus drove on, or the track the train carried you along on. Not to mention all those involved in making that vehicle or train or plane or boat that you travel in, or the building in which you work or go to school in, or the home that you live in. Or the breakfast, or lunch, or dinner, or snacks you eat throughout each day.

NONE OF THIS IS POSSIBLE WITHOUT THE HELP OF HUNDREDS, IF NOT THOUSANDS, OF STRANGERS!!!

None of us gets through one day without the help and cooperation of a web of humanity all pulling together.

And yes, I know it doesn't look like we're all pulling together on the outside. Yes, I know that guy cut you off, and that person cut in line, and the other person looked at you funny or stole your seat, or, or, or, or every news story about the horrors of humanity that will be on the television or most of the social media sites tonight.

But NONE of those things negates what I just said. We cannot get through our days without the help of others, seen or unseen. And that is a fact.

"Woah, woah, woah, Lee. What about people living off the grid? I've got you there. They get through their days totally self-reliant."

No, actually, they don't. Not unless they were born out of thin air and use only tools that they fashioned themselves and are doing it in their birthday suits or some leaves that they somehow pulled together. Because if they have on clothes, if they are using tools, if they were taught how to survive, the supplies, the knowledge, the materials all came from strangers who maybe, just maybe aren't quite as ill-willed and dangerous as some might have us believe.

As you know from an earlier chapter, I was a professional firefighter/paramedic. I can tell you from experience that the idea that the truth of an individual comes out in desperate circumstances is quite true. And I can tell you it is nearly impossible for me to remember a wreck that I arrived at or a fire that I fought, where strangers weren't assisting when we arrived.

But let's not stick to just my experiences, let's take the most desperate circumstance that the whole world is aware of in modern times and see what was there. Of course, I'm referring to the events of 9/11. And I don't even have to say more than that for you to know *exactly* what event I am referring to, as it affected every one of us of age on the planet.

It wasn't just America that grieved; it wasn't just Americans that came rushing to help. Strangers from all around the world pulled together.

The best of humanity came out, not the worst. Superheroes came from around the world to help sift through the ashes. They wrote songs and poems and did acts of kindness for people they had never known. They donated money, they said prayers, they flew an American flag alongside their own. There were no Republicans or Democrats in the US, there were no races; there were only Americans. And around the world, there was the same.

9/11 is far from the only example of this. Hurricanes on islands and across the coast, wildland fires in dry areas, flooding, tornadoes, earthquakes, and natural disasters of all shapes and sizes are all always followed by troops and troops of superhero strangers, pulling on their capes and reaching out to help.

The bottom line is simple. When humanity is truly pressed, its survival truly threatened, strangers don't become dangers—they become brothers and sisters … and superheroes emerge.

CHAPTER 10
EXERCISING ADMIRATION OF STRANGERS

I'm going to start this chapter, perhaps a little different from you might have thought I would. I'm going to start it with an admission. The admission is this—yes, I know that not all strangers are superheroes. It hurts me to say it. But yes, the evidence is easy to see. The hate, the fear, the "me first" islands of one that some live on. Their drive to dominate all others. Yes, I know it's there. I do see it, too.

And sure, I'll admit that at this current moment on our planet, there might just be more of that going on than what I ended the last chapter with.

BUT SO WHAT???

You want to go and find the bad in the world, that's easy. Just turn on the news or scroll through most social media platforms. Just watch a political pundit, listen to a sports analyst, or even a wardrobe or food or movie or vehicle analyst, or, or, or whatever critic blasting about how the other person is wrong, isn't good enough, isn't more enough. Sure, it's everywhere.

And again, I say, SO WHAAAAAAAT???

There's nothing special or superhero about being able to see what is everywhere. What is seemingly obvious to all. And *this* is a book for superheroes. It takes the vision of a superhero to see past all that garbage and find the beauty worth admiring. And that's what they do, don't they? In our comics and in our movies, over and over and over again, they refuse to see the destruction, the fighting, the selfishness. Instead, they use their super-vision to see past the hard outer shells to the soft underbelly of what is worth fighting for; the seed of goodness and possibility and hope that lies within everyone around them. They see the truth, not the lies it is cloaked in. And since you are a superhero, that is exactly what you are going to do on this next exercise.

For the next three days, or five days, or seven days, (your choice), you are to work out your admiration muscle *on strangers* each day.

Remember, it's important that whatever number of days you pick, stick to it all the way to the end. You can still use your stick-to-it-ive-ness superpower to keep going. And, as always, if you fall down, (accidentally skip a day), don't worry about that. We know that all superheroes fall down and that they all get back up, too, and so can you.

EXERCISE:

Each day, as you go about your day, notice what others get *right*. If you're not working, go for a walk outside, or if weather doesn't permit, walk in a mall and notice things about strangers that are *right*. If travel outside <u>truly</u> isn't possible on one day, don't even skip that day, instead go on social media and do the exercise there. One way or another, observe others and find what is *right* about them.

It could be that they have actual clothes on their body. That they seem to have brushed their teeth and don't have any food stuck between them, or, if they do have food stuck between them, that they seem to be able to carry on anyway.

It could be that they held open a door for someone or hurried just enough to catch the train or the bus. It could be that they've lost everything in the world and are homeless but are caring for a dog.

It could be that they stay up for hours on end, driving big, long-haul trucks to deliver goods or groceries to stores. That they have a nice smile or laugh or hair or bald head. It could be that they are bold enough to wear flashy shoes or a cowboy hat. That they brought you the correct lunch order or that they knew all those names for coffee concoctions. That they swept the floors to keep your office or school building clean. That they picked up the trash in front of your and your neighbor's and a few hundred other neighbor's houses and kept the streets from becoming diseased.

It could be that they are a firefighter and are willing to risk their life for any stranger in their district. Or that they are a police officer and are willing to do that for little to no thanks. It could be that they are serving and protecting your country by serving in the armed forces or that they are back home serving your children at the school or you at your church.

The fact is it could be as many different things as there are people and pro-survival actions that people can take. The only limit on finding things to admire is how big your superhero admiration muscle actually is. And however big or small it may be right now, as with all exercises, muscles exercised do get bigger and faster and better overall, and so can your superhero admiration muscle.

The important thing about doing this exercise isn't what you notice about others that is right, it's that you DO the exercise. Keep noticing their kindnesses or perseverance, their ability to do the right thing; whatever is right about them. And throughout the day, or at the end of the day, write down as many as you can, but at least five.

Who knows, you might even start to feel like we aren't all quite doomed for eternity. You might even crack a smile about others, or maybe even a laugh of wonderment.

At the end of each day, if you think you haven't been able to find even one thing that others got right, remember that they also made it to that moment. And write down a description of at least five people that you saw that day. Write down what you imagine that they might be struggling with in their own lives. And then write down that at least they were able to continue through the last moment that you saw them today.

And if that doesn't help you to see THAT as something to be admired about them, then go back and read Chapter 7 all over again, again. As a matter of fact, anytime that you come to the end of your day while doing this exercise and can't find at least five things to write down that others got right, go back and reread Chapter 7—again, again. Then come back here and write down at least one thing that you can admire about at least one person in your life.

> **NOTE:** Just like in our previous exercise, it is possible that you might feel a little worse when you first start than before you began. Don't worry about it, ignore the butter-flies in your stomach or continual chatter of what is wrong with others that might be going on in your head and just keep going. Remember, most of the social structures in our current world have not been continu-ally teaching you to exercise your admi-ration muscle. In fact, many of them have been trying to convince you that you don't have one. But you've been working it up over the last couple of exercises, so you're getting stronger and it's getting more used to being used again. Keep going, the sore-ness will continue to work out and, like the runner who increases his runs from one mile, to two miles, and then to three miles,

it can be done.

IMPORTANT NOTE: If you find that you just can't do this exercise, that you feel like you are just lost or stopped on it, DON'T GIVE UP! You may have just "run too fast."

I'll explain.

As any athlete can tell you, muscles have to be properly conditioned with a proper base in before they can handle the next increase in activity.

Your admiration muscle is no different. If you simply can't do this exercise, and none of the above solutions will work to help you push through to feeling good about it, then you just didn't get enough of a base in on the last exercise. Maybe you only did three days when your muscle actually needed seven days. Maybe you did seven but didn't really fully understand what you were doing when you started, so you didn't truly get in a *full* seven days.

Whatever the reason, the solution is simple. Just go back two chapters, to chapter eight. Reread that chapter, then chapter nine with the exercise, and either extend your days on the exercise or redo the full seven days on the exercise, if that is how many you did before. Your superhero muscle *will* condition if you use it the amount it needs to get in the base. So, use your stick-to-it-ive-ness and get in the number of days *you* need to build the base of your admiration muscle to the next base before coming back through chapters nine and ten.

WHAT TO DO:

Throughout the day or at the end of each day, write down all the things that you noticed others got right. In other words, what they did that is worth admiring. Or simply skip to what you managed to admire about others today and write those things down.

Remember, it needs to be at least five per day, but you get extra superhero stars on your cape or tights or crown, or whatever it is that pleases you, for each of the strangers beyond those first three.

[**SARCASTIC NOTICE:** stars not included with purchase and must be purchased separately. Like you didn't already know that...]

[If you'd like a free pdf of this exercise, and all the rest of the exercises, to print out for easier writing, go to www.handbooksfor-superheroes.com and enter the passcode: someone.]

THINGS YOU ADMIRED ABOUT STRANGERS:

DAY ONE

_____

_____

DAY TWO

_____

_____

DAY THREE

_____

_____

DAY FOUR

_____

_____

DAY FIVE

_____

_____

DAY SIX

_____

_____

DAY SEVEN

_____

_____

DAY EIGHT

_____

_____

DAY NINE

_____

_____

DAY TEN

_____

_____

Did you complete your selected number of days on the exercise, with or without having to go back and retread some of the previous chapters?

Great, either way!

Well done!

It's time for the next step!

CHAPTER 11

TREES AND FELLOW SUPERHEROES

Do you know what the oldest living organism discovered on earth is? Outside of a few bacteria and other microbes, it's a tree. On the surface it is many, many trees that cover over 100 acres. But underneath the ground they share a root system that scientists say operates as one organism, because it connects to all of them and is the foundation from which they grow. The group of trees is called *Pando*, or the *Trembling Giant*, and is located in a national forest in the state of Utah, in the USA.

Scientists say that they know it is at least 80,000 years old and could be up to 1 million years old. Apparently, it's quite difficult to determine the exact age of the root system. But the point is that sucker has been alive for a very long time! Longer than anything else they can find that doesn't pretty much take a microscope to see that it's alive.

Not only is it the oldest, it's also the heaviest living organism in the world, weighing in at over a whopping 6,600 tons. By comparison the average U.S. car weighs about 2 tons. So, it would take 3,300 of those cars to add up to the weight of ole *Pando*.[4]

You know what else is interesting about trees in general?

THEY TALK TO EACH OTHER!!!

For real! They do!

Apparently, even giraffes know this!

"Okay, Lee, you've lost me. First off, only the trees in the Wizard of Oz and Avatar and Lord of the Rings talk. Secondly, since when did this become a science book??? I want self-help!"

Well, one, I think you may need help with that anger, the way you keep attacking me. Perhaps that will be my next book. Probably not. Try skipping or riding tricycles; it will help. Two, how can you not want to know about giraffes and trees???

Anyway, stop distracting me.

4https://www.mitchellrepublic.com/lifestyle/home-and-garden/4526947-are-trees-communicating-research-says-yes (date accessed July 1. 2020)

Back to my point.

Scientists have found that trees send chemical, hormonal, and slow-pulsing electrical signals to each other through their network of root systems and microscopic fungal filament (just think of it as a massive spider's web that is microscopic). They call the whole system the "wood-wide web."

Seriously. It's a thing. Google it. The trees use this system to share nutrients and help each other with growth, such as larger trees that can get to the sunlight in a forest to turn the heat into sugars for energy, sharing that sugar with the little trees that are still trying to grow up under their cover. Or the exchange of carbon for sugar energy between the trees and the fungal filament (you remember, that microscopic spider's web stuff).

They also even talk to each other through the air to warn each other of animals like giraffes eating away at their leaves! They do this by sending different scented hormones (pheromones) into the air for the other trees to pick up on or smell or hear or whatever it is they do to receive the communication.

To be specific, when a giraffe starts eating away at the leaves on a tree, the tree will put out a distress signal in the form of ethylene gas into the air. When the trees around it receive this communication, they will start pumping bitter chemical compounds called tannins into their leaves. In large quantities these tannins will sicken or even kill a giraffe who eats them.

The giraffes are so aware of this that when grazing into a group of this types of trees, they will do it into the wind, so that the warning gas doesn't get blown over to the trees it's working toward eating the leaves on next! Oh, and when there is no wind at all, they will graze on one tree and then typically walk about 100 yards away to start eating the next one, which is farther than the gas the tree released can travel in the air to warn the other trees![5]

Amazing, right?! And, and, this analogy translates perfectly into when the superheroes all band together to fight off the evil, side by side!

"What?!"

Seriously, you need to do something about that temper. In the meantime, I'll explain.

---

5 Richard Grant. "Do Trees Talk to Each Other?" Smithsonian.com, Smithsonian Institution, 1 Mar. 2018, www.smithsonianmag.com/science-nature/the-whispering-trees-180968084/. (date accessed July 1. 2020)

CHAPTER 11

When the superheroes all band together to fight off evil, they work together great! They communicate with each other and are a great teeeeeeaammmm... mmmaaaattteessssssss......

Wait, a second. That's not what they do at all, is it?

They're usually pretty self-centered about their own agendas, when they first come together. They often don't want to be there with some of the other superheroes, in the first place. Sometimes they don't even want to be with *any* of the other superheroes. They get in fights. One usually leaves, if not several of them. And typically there's at least one that's new at it and not sure of his or her superpowers yet, or that they even belong among the other superheroes. I guess they're not like trees at all. They don't really talk *to* each other at all. Funny little quips sometimes. But mostly it's *at* one another. Plus, there're no giraffes ...

My analogy of my first analogy sucks.

OR DOES IT???

You see, the superheroes seem to always start off that way, but at the end, when the stakes start getting really high, when the supervillain is really pressing in, when humanity really, really needs them, they all start seeing strengths in the other superheroes. Little quirks like, oh, I don't know, becoming big and green and angry or shooting spiderwebs from their wrists or going invisible are all of a sudden seen as things to admire, instead of fear. And always, always, it takes the whole team pulling together to defeat the enemy!

They go from talking *at* each other to talking *to* each other. They become a team of connected trees and beat those giraffes from eating them, and all of humanity, up!

BOOOOOOOM!!

Analogies connected!! I wordsmithed the crap out of that! Ha!

Okay, so maybe they're not perfectly connected, but I do think you get my point, right?

When we want to survive, we have to stay connected; we have to work together. While we may be individual trees or superheroes standing alone, underneath it all we are so much stronger when we operate as a connected unit. When we see each other's strengths instead of weaknesses.

Unfortunately, too much of humanity seems to

have been convinced to pretend to be separated. Convinced to believe in stranger danger everywhere. Some seem to focus only on their own goals and purposes. They seem to fight to get to the sunlight before the other trees can or to stand in the light to block out the other superheroes so that all glory can be theirs alone.

But just as the wood-wide web in the forest is keeping it alive, it is humanity's connectedness that keeps it surviving. Living in islands of one isn't sustainable. And, as we covered before, none of it is really even possible without the help of others.

CHAPTER 12

EXERCISING REHABBING THE WORD-WIDE WEB OF HUMANITY

After 30 years of research in Canadian forests, Scientist Suzanne Simard says she has discovered that not only are the trees connected and talking to each other, she has identified the larger, older trees as hub trees, or *mother trees,* as she prefers to call them. She dubs them this, not because of female or male connotation, but because of how they help take care of the smaller trees around them.

You see, these trees have survived a lot. They have knowledge and insight that the little trees starting out haven't acquired yet. Plus, they are really tall and stable and can get plenty of sunlight to convert into energy.

Suzanne says that if loggers take out these trees or tear up their root system, then the survival chances of the little trees around them drops immensely.[6]

This is similar to what happens to our world when the superheroes are taken out. The super-heroes see what's best in humanity, not what is worst. They have endured longer, they are bigger and stronger both physically and where it counts even more, through the eyes of the heart.

And when they train those eyes on the humans around them, they reflect the beauty that is inside those people and really make them want to be more, because they remind them of what is *right* about them.

This is important to keep in mind as we move into this next exercise and begin to rebuild the *word*-wide web that supports us all.

You see what I did there? Huh? Huh? See, I took the "wood-wide web" of forests and word-smithed it to be the "*word*-wide web" of humanity. Man, I'm on a roll!

Pretty cool, right?

6 Diane Toomey, *Yale Environment 360*, September 1, 2016. "Explor-ing How and Why Trees 'Talk' to Each Other." e360.yale.edu/features/ exploring_how_and_why_trees_talk_to_each_other. (date accessed July 1. 2020)

Never mind; back to my point.

You see, when those *mother trees* and super-heroes send a communication to the smaller ones around them, they have a strong intention both for that communication to arrive to the one they are sending it to *and* for that one to survive better because of it.

While that may sound complicated, it's actually not. Well, not for you, since you are a superhero. In fact, you already do this all the time.

I'll show you.

Have you ever helped a child that scraped their knee, or lost their teddy bear? Have you held the door open for an elderly person with a friendly, "Let me get that for you, sir or ma'am?" Have you squeezed someone you love tight and told them it would be okay? Have you shared a joke with a friend and smiled bigger when they laughed? Have you let a stranger merge in traffic, with a little wave? Have you checked a ballot box in a voting booth? Have you explained how to deal with a math problem or language problem or history problem to another classmate? Have you paid for the customer's coffee or meal behind you at a drive-through window?

Each of these interactions are not just phys-ical. Like with the trees there is energy being exchanged in that communication. And just as with those trees, with each of your interactions you are contributing to the furthering of the sur-vival of what you are agreeing with and commu-nicating to. You are saying, "Go on, keep going, you deserve to live, I agree with your idea, I think there is something *right* about you."

And that is what we are going to do in this next exercise of rebuilding the *word*-wide web.

Yeah, that's not going away.

Okay, I'll focus.

On this exercise we aren't going to say all of those things implied above, we are just going to say hi, hello, howdy, ciao, hola, privet, ni hau, kon-nichiwa, bonjour, salut, hallo, buon giorno, salaam, namaste, or however it is that you communicate a friendly greeting to another in your country, state, city, province, or town. You are welcome to also use my grandmother's very friendly "Hi-dy" combo of hi and howdy, if you're feeling short on options.

For the next three days, or five days, or seven days, (your choice), you are to say a friendly hello type of greeting to at least three strangers per day. It could be 10 strangers. It could be 100 strangers. There is no limit on how many, but it must be at least three. The important thing is that whatever number of days you pick, stick to it all the way to the end. Remember, you can use your stick-to-it-ive-ness superpower to keep going. And, as always, if you fall down, (accidentally skip a day), don't worry about that. We know that all superheroes fall down and that they all get back up too, and so can you.

EXERCISE:

Each day, as you go about your day, say a friendly hello type of greeting to three or more strangers.

It is important to keep in mind your previous exercises. Remember to be in present time. If you are having trouble with that, find some things in the environment that you admire that help you be in present time. Take a second to admire yourself for doing this exercise. Then find something you admire about a stranger and then say hello to them. This could take a minute or more, or it could all happen in a matter of seconds.

Remember, anything that you can see in

another and feel like you could approve of, be pleased about, or in an actual state of wonderment about qualifies as something you admire. You don't have to make a big deal out of it, just notice it. It will give you that inner smile to greet them with when you send your hello.

For sure, there will be some people who look at you weird or think you're crazy or don't respond. Remember that often parts of humanity turn on the superheroes. They don't believe enough in their own goodness to believe that the superhero has any, or sometimes that the superheroes exist at all.

Heck, as we've already covered, even the superheroes themselves didn't all get along when they first got together. Many were fighting their own battles to survive, just like a number of the strangers that you will come across.

You will be saying hello to humanity, to other superheroes that may or may not be aware of their own superpowers. So, the responses may vary greatly. But the important thing in this exercise isn't that you get a hello back, or even a smile back. The important thing is that you DO the exercise. Your superhero muscles have been being built up on the previous exercises. Just keep using them and they will keep growing.

Use your super kindnesses and persever-ance, your ability to do the right thing, no matter the responses you receive. By the end of your selected days I'm pretty confident that you'll start to see that perhaps humanity isn't quite doomed for eternity. You might even crack a smile about it, or maybe even start to see some wonderment in those you are sharing this planet with.

NOTE: Just like in our previous exercises, it is possible that you might feel a little worse when you first start than before you began. Don't worry about it, ignore the butterflies in your stomach and just keep going. Like the runner's sore body muscles have to be loosened up and conditioned, so does this superhero communication muscle. Espe-cially when nearly everyone around you is fighting the same archnemesis that you are.

IMPORTANT NOTE, AGAIN: If you find that you just can't do this exercise, that you feel like you are just lost or stopped on it, DON'T GIVE UP! You may have just "run too fast, again."

As we covered before, any athlete can tell you muscles have to be properly conditioned with a proper base built up in them before they can handle the next increase in activity. And your superhero admiration muscle is now having your superhero verbal communication muscle added to it.

So, if you simply can't do this exercise, and you've already gone back and reread chapter seven again and it didn't help you push through to feeling good about this, then you just didn't get enough of a base in on the last exercise.

Like before, maybe you only did three days when your muscle actually needed seven days. Or maybe you did seven but didn't really fully understand what you were doing when you started and so you didn't truly get in a full seven days.

Whatever the reason, the solution is, again, super simple. Just go back two chapters, to chapter ten. Reread that chapter, then chapter eleven with the exercise, and either extend your days on the exercise or redo the full seven days on the exercise, if that is how many you did before.

Your superhero muscle will condition if you use it the amount it needs to get in the proper base. So, use your stick-to-it-ive-ness and get in the number of days *you* need to build the base of your admiration muscle to the next base level before coming back through chapters eleven and twelve.

WHAT TO DO:

Throughout the day or at the end of each day, be in present time, notice something you admire about a stranger, and say hello to them in some fashion. In the spaces below, write down something that you admired about each of the persons you said hello to.

Remember, it needs to be at least three per day, but again, you get extra superhero stars on your cape or tights or crown, or whatever it is that pleases you, for each of the strangers beyond those first three.

[**SARCASTIC NOTICE, AGAIN:** stars not included with purchase and must be purchased separately. Like you didn't' already know that...]

[If you'd like a free pdf of this exercise, and all the rest of the exercises, to print out for easier writing, go to www.handbooksfor-superheroes.com and enter the passcode: someone.]

STRANGERS YOU SAID HELLO TO AND WHAT YOU ADMIRED ABOUT THEM:

DAY ONE

_____

_____

DAY TWO

_____

_____

DAY THREE

_____

_____

DAY FOUR

_____

_____

DAY FIVE

_____

_____

DAY SIX

_____

_____

DAY SEVEN

_____

_____

DAY EIGHT

_____

_____

DAY NINE

_____

_____

DAY TEN

_____

_____

Did you complete your selected number of days on the exercise?

Great!

Well done!

I admire you for making it through this step!!

CHAPTER 13

YOU'RE STILL THAT AWESOME . . .
AND SO ARE THEY

Remember when you were a kid and everything you did was so awesome that you had to rush to tell your parents or your best friend about it?

Me neither. But I do remember watching my kids growing up. I do remember how often I heard the words, "Dad! Watch this!" or "Dad! Look what I did!" or "Dad! Dad! Dad! Dad! Look at what I can do!"

You've seen this too, right? The excitement and continual sense of wonderment that a child has for what they can do, what they can create, what they are? Have you ever caught a child making faces at themselves in a mirror and laughing? If not, there's this thing called YouTube. I'm pretty sure you could find it there. Wherever you see it, is there anything better than that???

I really don't think there is. It certainly puts me in a state of wonderment; a state of true admiration. One of my aunts loves to tell this story about my little brother and me, from when we were kids. She says that we had gotten new tennis shoes from K-Mart or something. Our family didn't have much money when we were little. But as with most kids that age, we weren't aware of it and didn't really care. Our parents did an extraordinary job taking care of us, and we thought our new shoes were the coolest on the planet.

My aunt says that both my brother and I came running up to her shouting, "Aunt Patrice, look at my new shoes!!" Pointing and hopping to give her a better look, of course.

And there was no way it was ending at that. "They make me go so much faster!" we bragged to her. "Watch!" we shouted, before dashing off down the sidewalk, and then dashing proudly back, before strutting about like a peacock in all our new shoes and super-speed grandeur.

We were sooooo cool that we were in a state of wonderment of ourselves and our shoes.

And you know what? We're still that cool. And so are you!

I think we've already covered what society can often do to many kids like that by the time they are out of high school. And there's no need to rehash that or add to the seriousness pressure that gets piled on when you're older and there's a house or apartment to pay rent or a mortgage on. When the game of being an adult begins and all the play of life seems to diminish to fleeting glimpses as we rush to DO MORE, BE MORE.

No, we've covered that. So, let's instead focus on what might still be present in that "serious and driven, model citizen." And I'll start with this. Have you ever been walking into a store, or down the street, or anywhere else, lost in the worries of your world and been interrupted by a stranger's voice saying, "Nice shirt!" or "I like that hat," or "Oh, I love that purse!" or "Wow, those are great boots! Where did you get them?" Have you ever had that happen to you, or some version of it?

It's pretty amazing the effect it can have on you, isn't it? Here you are, lost from present time, your mind worrying away over past actions or future threats, and some stranger's kindness and admiration pulls you right out of the supervillain-ous hypnotic trance of worry and pops you right into the present moment. Not to mention the way it makes you smile. Even though sometimes only on the inside.

But other times it can be so powerful of a superhero move by the stranger that it breaks the hypnotic worry spell for more than a moment. Sometimes you walk a little taller, as the little superhero in you gets a chance to shine again.

Sure, it doesn't always work. There are also times when it barely breaks your trance. But somewhere, deep down, it does make you *right*. You do know that you can do something that is worth admiring. And while the peacock strut you might have broken into as a little kid may not fully come out, a little hope does make its way into your world.

You see, the truth is that not much has changed from when you were little and thought you were awesome. You are still that awesome, and so is that stranger you pass on the bus or on the walk into your building or on the elevator at work or in the hallway at school.

You know what I used to say back to my kids, when they asked me to watch something they were doing or look at something they had done? "Wow! That's awesome!" And then I'd watch them preen around like peacocks, just like I did when I was little.

Maybe one of the main things wrong with this world is that we stopped telling each other how awesome we are. Maybe we've spent so much time being told we were wrong, or not enough of whatever image we were supposed to live up to, that we finally started to believe it.

But I'll tell you what's more important than that, it's that the little peacock still resides in all of us. Sure, it's more buried in some than in others. But it's there. Just waiting for enough rightness to be noticed to start preening about all over again.

And what's more is that a world of happy, proud peacocks might be a little more fun than the serious, demanding one that too many of the talking heads on our screens keep insisting that we create and live in. Superheroes unite! It's time to shift the tide! Peacocks are waiting. And they're awesome!

CHAPTER 14

EXERCISING YOUR ADMIRATION/ COMMUNICATION MUSCLES ON THEIR AWESOMENESS

Remember when you did the exercise on finding things that you admire about others? That was really fun, wasn't it? Well now you get to supersize that exercise and send a communication along the *word*-wide web of how much you think that tree's leaves are gorgeous. Or how much you admire how tall it has grown.

Yes, sometimes those trees will ignore you, just like they did when you said hello. And yes, sometimes they will look at you like there is something wrong with you; like you probably have an axe or chainsaw behind your back.

They've had a lot of loggers come speak to them before with kind words, before chopping away at their magnificence. So sometimes they're not quick to trust.

You are following the analogy, right? See, the

trees are the people you'll be talking to on the word-wide web, instead of the wood-wide web. They used to be proud little peacocks, but they had their feathers pruned and got laughed at. They were told to put them away and be quiet and stand in line, and ...

Geez, I really can't stay away from the metaphors, can I? Well you know what? I don't care! That's how I do my peacock strut!! Ha!

All right, I think you get the point.

Now for the exercise.

For the next three days, or five days, or seven days, (your choice), you are to notice something that you admire about a stranger and tell them; at least three per day. As in our last exercise, it could be ten strangers. It could be 100 strangers. There is no limit on how many, but it must be at least three.

Again, it's important that whatever number of days you pick, you stick to it all the way to the end. Remember, just as in all the exercises before, you can use your stick-to-it-ive-ness superpower to keep going. And, as always, if you fall down, (accidentally skip a day), don't worry about that. We know that all superheroes fall down and that they all get back up too, and so can you.

EXERCISE:

Each day, as you go about your day, give a friendly compliment of something you admire to three or more strangers.

It is important to keep in mind all of our previous exercises. Remember to be in present time. If you are having trouble with that, find some things in the environment that you admire that helps you be in present time. Then admire yourself for being the awesome little peacock, superhero you are. *Then* find something you admire about a stranger and then tell that to them. Like the previous drill, this can take minutes or seconds, and either one is right.

Remember, anything that you can see in another and feel like you could approve of, be pleased about, or in an actual state of wonderment about qualifies as something you admire. You don't have to make a big deal out of it, just notice it. It will give you that inner smile to share with them as you let them know that they are *right* about something, at least in your eyes, if no one else's.

As we know by now, the responses may vary greatly. But the important thing in this exercise isn't that you get some sort of acknowledgement back, although much of the time you will. The important thing is that you DO the exercise. Your superhero muscles have been being built up for a while now. They are strong enough to take any pushback. Just keep using them.

Use your super kindnesses and perseverance again, your ability to see the inner peacock, even if it's hidden or dirty and covered by a hard shell. You know, because it's a turtle, with peacock feathers inside its shell.

Aaaaaany who, by the end of your selected days I'm pretty confident that you'll start agreeing with me, if you don't already, that humanity isn't quite doomed for eternity. You might even crack a smile about it, or maybe even start to see some wonderment in those you are sharing this planet with. Heck, you might even get your own strut back.

Go on with ya bad self—it's peacock time!

NOTE: Just like in our previous exercises, it is possible that you might feel a little worse when you first start than before you began.

Don't worry about it, ignore the butterflies in your stomach and just keep going. Like the runner's sore body muscles have to be loosened up and conditioned, so does this super-combo superhero admiration and communication muscle. Especially when nearly everyone around you is fighting the same self-invalidation archnemesis as you are.

IMPORTANT NOTE, AGAIN: You remember. If you just can't get past this one. Back up and reread two chapters before and redo that exercise until you get that muscle base in for *you.*

WHAT TO DO:

Throughout the day or at the end of each day, be in present time, notice something you admire about a stranger and tell them about it in some fashion. In the spaces below, write down the something that you admired in that person that you made *right.*

Remember, it needs to be at least three per day, but, as in our last two exercises, you get extra superhero stars on your cape or tights or crown, or whatever it is that pleases you, for each of the strangers beyond those first three. Or if you'd prefer, you can get extra peacock feathers this time.

[**SARCASTIC NOTICE:** stars (and now peacock feathers, as well) are not included with purchase and must be purchased separately. Like you didn't already know that...]

[If you'd like a free pdf of this exercise, and all the rest of the exercises, to print out for easier writing, go to www.handbooksforsuperheroes.com and enter the passcode: someone.]

STRANGERS YOU ADMIRED AND WHAT YOU TOLD THEM.

DAY ONE

_____

_____

DAY TWO

_____

_____

DAY THREE

_____

_____

DAY FOUR

_____

_____

DAY FIVE

_____

_____

DAY SIX

_____

_____

DAY SEVEN

_____

_____

DAY EIGHT

_____

_____

DAY NINE

_____

_____

DAY TEN

_____

_____

Did you complete your selected number of days on the exercise?

Great!

Well done!

I admire you for making it through this step!!

CHAPTER 15

TALKING TO SOMEONE . . .
AND NOT DYING

When you have a disagreement with some-one you really care about and decide that you want to mend that relationship, what is the most important thing you can do to fix it? Admit you were wrong? Prove you were right? Buy flow-ers? A dinner? Give a card?

Maybe those things will help. Well, except for the "prove you were the right one." But no relationship gets mended without talking *to* that person. You see, what we've been working on throughout this book is, in fact, something you already know how to do. It's something you have done over and over and over again throughout your existence. It's part of the superheroness that *is* you. Your ability to communicate to another, to reach them, to talk *to* them.

"No, Lee. I've never talked *to* anyone."

Well, now you're just delusional. I don't know

how to write about that. I guess try skipping and tricycles again and call me in the morning.

Anyway, back to my analysis of you. For example, let's take a time when you've helped a friend that was upset. You made sure to go be where they were at, in present time. And even if travel to their specific location on this planet wasn't possible, and you did it over the phone or internet, you were still *there* for them and you were still in present time, while doing it.

You noticed things about them, their sadness, their grief, or fear. You didn't focus on those things. You didn't make them wrong for those things. But you did want them to return to feeling better. You knew of their smile, their laugh, their care for others. You remembered how strong they were. You knew they could persevere and arrive to their goals and dreams, or at least the next moment and the one after that.

You knew they mattered and were worth giving life to. You knew you approved of them existing, that you were pleased that they were around, and that many times you had felt a sense of wonder over them and their friendship with you. In other words, you knew that you admired many things about them, or simply that you admired them as a person.

CHAPTER 15

What's more, is that you wanted them to see these things about themselves and were sometimes shocked that they couldn't already. So, you held their hand, you let them cry on your shoulder, and when they were done, or sometimes even before they were done, you started to remind them of all the wonderful things that were *right* about them that you could see with your super-vision, but they couldn't right then.

You told them why they mattered. You reminded them they had superpowers, too. That they could carry on. That there was always hope for a brighter day.

All they have to do is look, up in the sky … wait, no, that's not it.

All they have to do is look into a friend's eye … or maybe even a stranger's. Who knows, they might not even die.

Weeeeell, you had to know that I was going to take it over the top before it ended, didn't you??? Ha!

Hopefully, you do get the point, my friend; my fellow superhero. But just in case it slipped past you in this moment, I'll surmise. You see, you've been talking *to* people your whole life, and if you are still reading this sentence now, you did not die. Many of the people you talked *to* were strangers, others were friends or family. But the action and result are still the same; you were in present time; you did find something that you admired and you did tell someone about this, aaaaaaaaand you did not die.

Of course, you know what that means—you must be a superhero!!

And we're back were we started all over again!!

Man, I love it when that happens!

In the final analysis, there may be plenty to find wrong with our world. But that is not the work of superheroes. Sure, just like the ones in our movies and our comic books, we will ALL fall down, me included. We will have days when we can't see the good. Days when we lose our faith in humanity and even in ourselves. Days when we see only the bad and can't stop ourselves from pointing it out, both in others and in ourselves.

BUT AGAIN I SAY, SOOOO WHAAAAT????!!!!

Superheroes aren't superheroes because they are perfect. None of them are. They are superheroes because they get back up. Because they gain their faith again. Because they find their hope in good and *right* and push forward in that direction. They refocus their strengths and try to grow to be better the next time. They do not wallow in the past or their failures, because to do so is truly the only way one can wind up a failure. And that is not the stuff of superheroes, or the stuff of *you*.

> **REALITY NOTE:** Most of us have spent much of our lives under the continual barrage of the supervillainous, hypnotic pressure to do more and be more. Not to mention the continual attack of our arch-nemesis, self-invalidation. This can create habits and patterns of thinking that seem to become a way of life.

HABITS CAN BE BROKEN. LIFE CAN BE CHANGED.

With that note in mind, should you find yourself faltering at this new superhero line of work more often than you'd care to, and if you'd like to become a stronger, faster, more powerful superhero, then I kindly suggest that you go back through this book, from beginning to end, three, five or seven more times. Your choice.

And if you'd like to help create a world full of superheroes to help you save it, then while you are retraining again, perhaps you could gift this book to three, five, or seven of your friends ... or strangers, and ask them to join you in rebuilding the *word*-wide web on this planet. Your choice.

It's been a real pleasure talking *to* you. And look at that, neither of us died.

Hmmm. Maybe there's something to this, my superhero friend.

Much Love,
Lee

P.S. If you're looking for a place to connect to others who like to see the good in the world, please join our growing community of positive thinkers on my new social networking platform www.pluscomm.com. I hope to see you there.

CPSIA information can be obtained
at www.ICGtesting.com
Printed in the USA
BVHW091021231120
593961BV00012B/103